THE CHANGING FACE OF
SPAIN

EDWARD PARKER
Author and photographer

HODDER
Wayland

an imprint of Hodder Children's Books

© 2002 White-Thomson Publishing Ltd

Produced for Hodder Wayland by

White-Thomson Publishing Ltd

2/3 St Andrew's Place

Lewes BN7 1UP

946

Editor: Anna Lee

Copy editor: Jason Hook

Designer: Christopher Halls at Mind's Eye Design, Lewes

Proofreader: Alison Cooper

Additional picture research: Shelley Noronha, Glass Onion Pictures

Published in Great Britain in 2002 by Hodder Wayland, an imprint of
Hodder Children's Books

British Library Cataloguing in Publication Date

Parker, Edward

   Changing Face of Spain

   1. Spain I. Title II. Spain 946

ISBN: 0 7502 3842 9

Printed and bound in Italy by G.Canale &C.S.p.A., Turin

Hodder Children's Books

A division of Hodder Headline Limited,

338 Euston Rd, London NW1 3BH

Acknowledgements

The publishers would like to thank
the following for their contributions
to this book: Rob Bowden - statistical
research; Nick Hawken - illustrations
on pages 7, 24, 26, 40 and 43; Peter
Bull - map on page 5. All
photographs are by Edward Parker
except: Camera Press 43; James Davis
Travel Photography 16; David
Cumming/Eye Ubiquitous 21;
Duncan Maxwell/Robert Harding
Picture Library 32; Oxford Scientific
Films 19; WTPix 1, 9, 35

Contents

1 Barcelona, Capital of Catalonia

Barcelona is the second-largest city in Spain and has a population of 1.5 million. In the last ten years, the city's economy, and much of its population, has enjoyed a boom in prosperity. Barcelona is the capital of Catalonia, which, like several other areas of Spain, has its own distinctive culture and language.

At the beginning of the twentieth century, Barcelona was one of the first Spanish cities to become industrialized. It fell into decline in the 1980s, but since 1990 the city has adapted well to changes in the world economy. Originally a city of heavy industry, and one of Spain's most important Mediterranean ports, it has developed into a city of high-tech industry and a major tourist destination.

Today, Barcelona is a thriving commercial centre. New, more environmentally friendly factories have been built by companies such as the SEAT car company, which is part of Spain's largest export sector of cars and car parts. Spanish exports to the rest of Europe have increased generally, and Barcelona, situated only 100 km from the French border, is in an ideal location for exporting.

Barcelona became one of Europe's most famous cities after hosting the hugely successful 1992 Olympic Games. In preparation for the Olympics, and with help from the European Union (EU), an Olympic Village rose from the disintegrating old industrial area of the city. Art galleries opened, the run-down dock area became a complex of restaurants and yachting marinas, and the historic centre of Barcelona was restored.

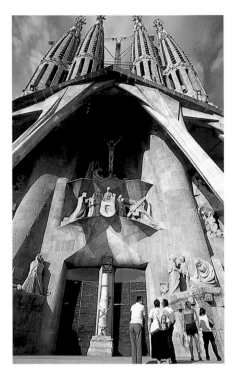

▲ La Sagrada Familia *church is an example of the striking architecture found in the wealthy city of Barcelona. It is a major attraction for the many tourists who visit Barcelona each year.*

▶ *Tourists crossing the new bridge that links the old city with the restaurants and entertainment centre in the renovated docks.*

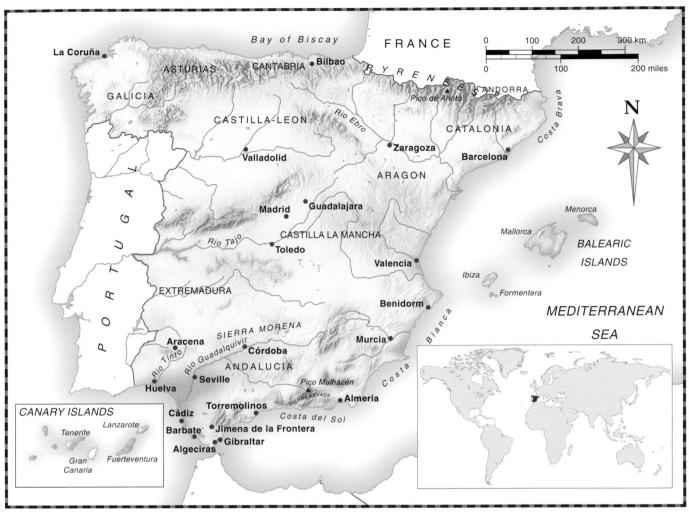

▲ *This map shows the main geographical features of Spain and places mentioned in this book.*

SPAIN: KEY FACTS

Area: Mainland Spain, 493,486 sq km; Balearic Islands, 4,992 sq km;
   Canary Islands, 7,447 sq km

Population: 39.5 million

Population density: 80 people per hectare

Capital city: Madrid (2.9 million)

Other main cities: Barcelona (1.5 million), Valencia (0.7 million), Seville (0.7 million)

Highest mountain: Pico de Mulhacén (3,478 m)

Longest river: Rio Tajo (1,007 km)

Main language: Spanish (other official languages include: Catalan, Valencian, Basque, Galician)

Major religion: Catholicism

Currency: Euro

Past and Present

A brief history

A series of invaders have left their mark on Spanish culture. The Romans occupied Spain for nearly 600 years, from 218 BCE, before being driven out by Germanic tribes. In CE 711 the Moors, a Muslim people from North Africa, invaded. The Moors governed southern Spain for nearly 800 years.

In 1492, Spanish Christians recaptured Granada, the last stronghold of the Moors. All non-Christians, including Moors and Jews, were expelled from the country. That same year, Christopher Columbus discovered the Americas, whose riches would make Spain one of the most powerful nations in the world.

▲ The huge cathedral in Seville was built by the Christians after the North African Moors had been expelled in the fifteenth century.

Recent developments

By the early 1900s, Spain had become divided into Left and Right political factions. These clashed in the Spanish Civil War of 1936–9. General Francisco Franco, the leader of the Right, emerged to take power. Franco would rule the country as dictator for the next thirty-six years.

▶ A range of international flags flutter in the wind in the main plaza of the town of Palos de la Frontera, where Christopher Columbus began his sea voyage to discover the Americas in 1492.

The death of Franco in 1975 marked the beginning of Spain's transformation into a modern European nation. Under King Juan Carlos, the country moved from dictatorship to democracy. In 1977, political parties and trade unions were legalized. Roman Catholicism ceased to be the official religion (although it is still widely practised), and divorce became legal. Spain's democratic government also gave greater independence to the country's seventeen regions. Today each one has its own parliament.

Spain joined the EU in 1986, and the national economy boomed. In the early 1990s Spain established a national health service, made improvements to the education system and raised the university population to over one million. By 2000, Spain had completed its transformation from one of the poorest and least industrialized countries in Europe to one of the major European economies.

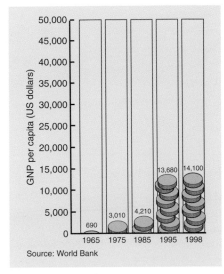

Source: World Bank

▲ *This graph shows the dramatic rise in Spain's gross national product from 1965 to 1998.*

IN THEIR OWN WORDS

'My name is Antonio Leon. I'm an agricultural engineer, and I work for the regional government of Andalucía. In this region we've received a lot of assistance from the European Union to help modernize our agriculture. My research is partly funded by the EU. I study soil types, and in this photo I'm testing soil near Seville.

'There have been many changes in Spanish agriculture over the past decade, especially since we joined the European Union. Some crops, such as sunflowers, are subsidized, and grants are available to install irrigation systems to grow fruit and vegetables intensively under plastic. This means that farmers can produce larger quantities of fruit, even when we haven't had much rain.'

3 | Landscape and Climate

Spain is the second-largest country in western Europe after France, and the second most mountainous country after Switzerland. The central plateau, or Meseta, occupies around 40 per cent of the country. It forms a vast tableland between 400 and 1,000 m above sea level. The Meseta is a sparsely populated area with a few main cities. It is split in two by the Cordillera Central mountain range, which rises to 2,400 m.

Mountains

The mountain ranges outside the Meseta are much higher and more rugged than the Cordillera Central. The Pyrenees, which run for 400 km along the French border, include a number of peaks over 3,000 m. The highest peak in this range is Pico de Aneto in Aragón, which is 3,408 m high. The Cordillera Bética, which includes Spain's highest peak, Mulhacén, stretches across southern and eastern Spain in the region of Andalucía.

▲ *The lush green slopes of the Pyrenees mountains in northern Spain are in the part of the country referred to as 'wet Spain'.*

IN THEIR OWN WORDS

'My name is Francisco Rabin and I have lived all my life in the village of Biescas in the Pyrenees. I love living in the mountains – I think this is one of the most beautiful places in Spain. However, living here we've also experienced some terrible natural disasters.

'In 1999, after the worst storm I've ever seen, a huge wave swept down the two rivers that run past the village. The high walls around the river saved the village from being flooded, but the wave was so powerful that it swept away a campsite south of Biescas. Many people lost their lives.'

Coasts and islands

Mainland Spain has 3,904 km of coastline, and more than 2,000 beaches. The Mediterranean coastline is famous for the sandy beaches that run from the Costa del Sol in the south to the Costa Brava in the north. Spain's Atlantic coastline is often rugged, and the sea temperatures are lower than those of the Mediterranean. The most well-known Spanish islands are the Canary Islands in the Atlantic Ocean, and the Balearic Islands – including Majorca and Ibiza – in the Mediterranean.

Lowlands

Between the main mountain ranges are five lowland areas: north-eastern Catalonia; the Ebro Basin south of the Pyrenees; Galicia in the north-west; the coastal plains around Valencia and Murcia; and the Guadalquivir river basin in central Andalucía.

▼ *The Mediterranean coast of Spain is famous for its clear waters.*

Climate

Spain has great variations in climate between its regions. It has mountain peaks that can remain covered in snow all year round, and a Mediterranean coastline that remains warm almost throughout the year. There is a huge contrast in rainfall between the wet regions of the north-west, and the arid conditions elsewhere. This has led to the country being divided into 'wet' and 'dry' Spain.

Wet Spain

The Pyrenees and the provinces facing the Bay of Biscay, from Galicia to the Basque country, bear the brunt of the cold north and north-westerly air streams. These bring heavy rainfall and moderate temperatures to around one-third of Spain. La Coruña, for example, receives more than 1,000 mm of rain annually. It has an average winter temperature of 10 °C, and moderate summer temperatures of around 20 °C.

▼ *Lush forests near Algeciras. Rainfall is much higher in forested regions than in other areas.*

The removal of large areas of forest has affected local climates. In the Parque de Alcornocales in Andalucía, some areas of remaining oak forest still receive up to 2,000 mm of rain each year (as much as a rainforest). A few kilometres outside the forest, rainfall can be below 300 mm.

Dry Spain

The huge, central Meseta receives around one-quarter of the rainfall that falls on the north-west coast, and cities such as Zaragoza and Valladolid receive less than 300 mm each year. Dry Spain experiences a continental climate, where the temperatures vary hugely between summer and winter. Madrid, for example, can reach over 35 °C in summer. However, it regularly has night-time winter temperatures below -10 °C.

▶ *These newly planted olives near Seville are irrigated using a drip irrigation system. Here, as in other parts of 'dry Spain', there is little rainfall for most of the year.*

IN THEIR OWN WORDS

'My name is Juan Espinosa and I live in a village called Gutierrez Muñoz about 100 km from Madrid. When I was young we used to grow mainly olives, wheat, and grapes for wine. Today the climate is much drier, and we have to irrigate some crops. Also, we now grow strawberries – in this picture I'm in a huge strawberry field. We irrigate the fruit during the hot summer months, then transport them to the south to ripen in Andalucía during the winter.'

4

Natural Resources

Minerals

Spain has a long history of mining, stretching back centuries. The country is particularly rich in iron ore, mercury, potash, pyrites and gold. The main coal and iron ore mines are located in the northern regions of the Basque country, Asturias and Cantabria. Deposits of lead and copper are mainly located in the southern region of Andalucía. Spain has some of the largest gold deposits in Europe. It is also one of the world's biggest producers of granite and marble, which are used in construction. Until recently, Spain has lacked major deposits of hydrocarbons such as coal and oil, but in the late 1990s a number of oil reserves were discovered under the Mediterranean.

▼ *Here zinc is being mined from one of the world's biggest opencast mines at Corta Atalaya.*

Seas and oceans

In the past, the coastal waters of Spain provided the country with a seemingly endless supply of fish. Unfortunately, Spain's waters have been severely overfished in the last thirty years. Some fish species have almost become extinct because of over-fishing, and the future of Spain's fishing industry depends on reducing and managing its fish catch.

▶ *A fishing boat leaves the port of Barbate. The Spanish love of seafood means that there is always a great demand for fish in Spain. This has led to problems with overfishing.*

IN THEIR OWN WORDS

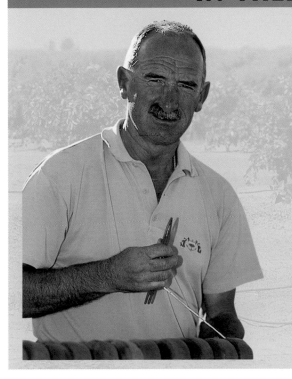

'My name is Pepe Gonzalez and I live in the small town of Barbate on the southern coast of Spain, near Cadiz. I've lived here all my life, and like my father I'm a fisherman. I work on a medium-sized fishing boat and we mainly catch sardines.

'I don't think people realize how important the ocean is for Spain. One of the main foods in the Spanish diet is fish, and the fishing industry employs a lot of people. We have to be careful to look after our seas and make sure that there'll always be a good supply of fish.'

Energy

Spain relies on imports for most of its oil and 50 per cent of its coal. It also relies heavily on importing natural gas from North Africa, with 70 per cent being supplied by Libya and Algeria via a pipeline under the Mediterranean.

Spain has concentrated on building a network of hydro-electric and nuclear power stations to meet its energy needs. The country has uranium deposits, and in 1999 nuclear power accounted for 29.5 per cent of the country's electricity generation. Spain is also investing in developing sustainable forms of energy, such as solar and wind power. Major wind farms have been established in Andalucía, and Spain is now one of the most advanced countries in Europe in this form of energy.

▲ *Wind farms for producing electricity, like this one near Tarifa, are becoming a familiar sight in southern Spain.*

IN THEIR OWN WORDS

'I'm José Luis García and I work for WWF, the environmental organization. We're campaigning for the use of alternative and sustainable forms of energy production. Spain has a large potential for changing from polluting oil and gas power stations to wind farms and small-scale solar power plants. Spain has more hours of intensive sunshine than most European countries, and in the future we hope that this will be exploited to produce more electricity.'

Forests

Many areas of natural forest have been cut down over the last 2,000 years, in order to make way for agriculture and to provide timber. But forests remain a major resource for a number of regions. In Andalucía and Extremadura, there are extensive cork-oak and holm-oak forests. The cork oaks provide a valuable harvest every nine years, and the holm oaks are vital to the huge pork industry. Every autumn, pigs are let loose in the forest to fatten up on acorns.

Around 33 per cent of Spain is covered by forest. The percentage is set to rise as the EU is helping to fund a reforestation plan. This will encourage farmers to convert agricultural land to commercial forests of pine and eucalyptus. The plan is designed to increase commercial forests by 153,000 hectares between 2001 and 2006, at a cost of 440 million euros.

▼ *Recently harvested cork oaks near Algeciras.*

Agricultural landscape

The agricultural landscape in many parts of Spain has changed dramatically since the country became part of the EU in 1986. Many arid areas have been made suitable for agriculture through subsidized irrigation schemes. The country's climate is well-suited to modern irrigated horticulture, and the production of fruit and vegetables has increased significantly. Around Almería, on the Mediterranean coast, thousands of hectares of former desert are now covered in polythene tunnels growing fruit and vegetables, which are sold to northern Europe during winter months.

On the central plateau, the traditional crops are cereals, grapes and olives. Today, Spain remains the world's main producer of olive oil. Some areas are being converted to sunflower crops to take advantage of EU subsidies.

▲ *Torremolinos, on the Costa del Sol, is one of several regions where plastic is used to protect vast areas of crops.*

Many of these crops are never harvested, because the subsidy is received simply for planting the crop. Fruits such as strawberries are also being cultivated under irrigated conditions on the cool Meseta. These are transported hundreds of kilometres to the hotter southern coast to ripen and provide winter fruit.

Despite much change, large areas of Spain still have an agricultural landscape based on that established by the Romans 2,000 years ago. Olive groves, vineyards, small wheat fields, herds of goats and pigs, and bulls for bullfighting, are still typical of regions such as Extremadura.

▶ *A generous subsidy from the European Union is available for the planting of sunflower crops.*

IN THEIR OWN WORDS

'My name is Francisco Horgelo Sanchez and I live near the city of Huelva, close to the border with Portugal. I have a small piece of land on which I grow some oaks for my pigs, some olive trees and a few chestnut trees. I also have some sheep. During the summer, I work as a cork-oak harvester, and I often travel over 250 km to work in Algeciras. Many things have changed in Spain over the past fifty years, but in this area cork harvesting has remained the same since I was young.'

5

The Changing Environment

Spain's environment is changing in many ways. In recent times, new agricultural techniques have caused deforestation and soil erosion. Many wetlands have been drained, and other areas have been flooded for hydroelectric power schemes. Such destruction of natural habitat could have a serious effect on the country's wildlife.

Fortunately, Spain is a big country with a relatively small population, so large areas of wilderness still exist. Here, the rarest of Spain's wildlife can find shelter. Since the 1980s, the Spanish have become increasingly environmentally aware. One result has been the expansion of Spain's protected areas. In 1981, there were just thirty-five protected areas covering a few thousand hectares. Now there are more than 400, covering an area more than ten times that size.

Biodiversity

Spain has the most varied wildlife in Europe, and is home to many rare species from both Europe and Africa. It also forms part of the world's great migratory route for millions of birds, as they travel between Europe and Africa. Wetlands such as Doñana National Park in Andalucía provide important stopovers during migration.

▼ *The desert near Almería is the largest in Europe and is continuing to grow every year, due to deforestation.*

Spain has an estimated 630 species of animals and birds, of which forty are considered endangered. Environmental groups have successfully campaigned for the conservation of some of the rarest species, including the brown bear, wolf, lynx and griffin vulture. There are also well over 8,000 species of plant in Spain and the Balearic Islands, of which about eighty are considered in danger of extinction.

▲ *The beautiful European wolf is one of several species that is under threat of extinction.*

IN THEIR OWN WORDS

'My name is Maria José Buisan and I work in Ordesa and Monte Perdido National Park, in the Pyrenees. Our park is one of the smallest in Spain, covering just 156 sq km. It has many types of habitat, from deciduous forests in the valleys to alpine meadows where flowers such as gentians grow. The park is an important refuge for migrating birds. It's also home to rare animals and birds, like the chamois and the bearded vulture. It's really important that we work hard to protect our endangered species, because Spain has some of the most beautiful wildlife in Europe.'

IN THEIR OWN WORDS

'My name is Francisco Ramon and I have lived all my life in Barcelona. When I was young, Barcelona was very dirty. The air was always smoky. When there was no wind, pollution from the steel mills was especially bad. Since the Olympic Games in 1992, the city centre has been cleaned up. Factories have either been closed down or moved out of town. It's much easier to breathe now!'

Urban pollution

Urban pollution is less of a problem in Spain than in most other European countries. But in industrial towns such as Huelva, petrochemical factories cause serious water and atmospheric pollution. Traffic pollution is a problem in cities such as Madrid and Barcelona. These cities have responded by improving train services for commuters, and reserving priority lanes for cars carrying more than one passenger.

▼ *Improving the Metro system in Madrid is just one of the measures being taken to help reduce pollution from motor vehicles in the city.*

Tourism

Over the past thirty years, hundreds of kilometres of Spanish beaches have been developed into tourist resorts. Delicate dune and wetland ecosystems have been destroyed, and replaced by high-rise buildings. Fortunately, areas along the Costa de la Luz were once owned by the military, which prevented their use as farms or resorts. Much of this land, including Doñana, has since been made into national parks. Environmental groups such as the WWF-Spain and local communities are campaigning for more sensitive tourist development and the setting up of protected areas. Nevertheless, pollution from the activities of nearly 50 million tourists every year is a major environmental problem.

▼ *Benidorm is one of the many places in Spain where wildlife has had to make way for tourism.*

Mining

Most of Spain's important mines are situated in two mountain ranges, the Cordillera Cantábrica and the Sierra Morena. These mines are a source of serious pollution. In 1998, the toxic metal settlement dam at the Aznalcollar Mine overflowed, and thousands of tonnes of toxic liquid ran in a huge wave along the Guadalquivir river valley. It came close to Spain's most important wetland, Doñana. The mountain location of mines means that pollution enters many water courses. Rivers such as the Rio Tinto are so contaminated that they support little or no life.

Changing habitat

Spain's low population density means that there are still large areas of forest and traditional agriculture. These are home to many species of plants and animals. But the forests are under threat of being made into commercial plantations of eucalyptus, which support very little wildlife.

▼ *Many areas of native oak and pine forest are being converted into fast-growing eucalyptus plantations using grants from the EU.*

In the last twenty years, improvements in irrigation systems have seen intensive farming increase dramatically. In areas where there is intensive agriculture, such as the Ebro river valley, pollution from pesticides and herbicides is a serious problem. Soil erosion is also severe. The 300 sq km Ebro delta is made up of soil that has been eroded from the Ebro's banks and carried down the river over hundreds of years.

IN THEIR OWN WORDS

'My name is Joaquin Gil Corrales and I live in the small town of Los Barrios near Algeciras. Here I am working in the cork-oak forest near my home. The hills around us are covered in cork-oak forest. In the spring, tens of thousands of birds fly over from Africa. Huge flocks turn the sky black. The birds are often so exhausted that when they land they fall asleep straight away. They spend a few days recovering their strength, and the forest is full of sleeping birds. I'm worried that plans to cut down some of the cork oak and plant eucalyptus instead might mean that the birds no longer come here.'

Water shortages

Nearly two-thirds of Spain is arid, and changes in the world climate in recent years have led to a number of serious droughts over the past twenty years. The huge areas that receive very little rainfall are heavily dependent on natural underground reservoirs. However, these reserves are being over-exploited for human use and for irrigating crops. Because of the increasing demand, water shortages are set to become more severe.

With the increasing demand from the urban populations and the increase in irrigation, many major rivers now have very low flows in the summer. Even the wetland at Doñana is at risk of drying up because of the increased use of underground water for irrigation.

▼ *In winter, this river near Seville can flood to as high as the watermark on the concrete wall near the top of the picture. However, during summer, the region suffers from water shortages.*

6

The Changing Population

At the beginning of the 1980s, Spain had one of the fastest-growing populations in Europe. Within twenty years the situation has completely changed. In 2000, Spain had the lowest average birth rate of any country in the world, at just 1.19 children per woman.

Spain was one of the last European nations to undergo the change from the high birth rate and death rate typical of rural societies, to the lower rates that characterize industrial societies. Today, Spain's population has a life expectancy (75 for men and 81 for women) that is better than most other countries in the EU. But the birth rate has fallen so sharply that Spain is predicted to have a declining population by the year 2010.

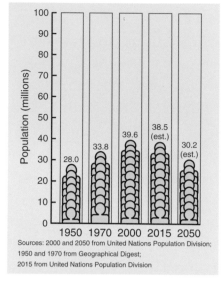

Sources: 2000 and 2050 from United Nations Population Division; 1950 and 1970 from Geographical Digest; 2015 from United Nations Population Division

▲ *This graph shows how population growth in Spain is predicted to decline.*

▼ *These young women are members of a generation that is predicted to have fewer children, and live longer, than ever before.*

IN THEIR OWN WORDS

'I'm Mariana Blasquez. I'm 15 years old and I live in the centre of Madrid. When I leave school, I'm going to study foreign languages at university. I want to travel and work abroad when I'm older, and then think about a career. I'd like to have children, but not until I'm about 30. I want to be free to travel before I have the responsibility of a family.

'I know I'm lucky to be able to choose what I want to do with my life. My parents married when they were only 20, but I want to make sure I enjoy myself before I settle down.'

In the 1960s, Spain had a very young population. But now, with an increase in life expectancy and a decrease in birth rate, the average age of the population is increasing. In 1975, just 10 per cent of the population was over 65. By 1999, this had risen to 14.8 per cent. Over the same period, the number of those under 15 dropped from 27.5 per cent to 18 per cent. One of the reasons for the decline is that women have far more career opportunities than ever before. Many are waiting until they are older before starting a family.

▲ These people live in a home for the elderly in Biescas, in the Pyrenees. In future, it may prove difficult for Spain to look after its ageing population, as there will be fewer workers paying the taxes needed to help support the elderly.

T030254

Migration

Towards the end of the Franco era, a huge number of people moved from the poor rural regions to the cities and tourist resorts. The cities developed shanty-towns to accommodate the migrants. In recent years, these have been replaced by high-rise tower blocks. Between 1959 and 1973, nearly 2 million Spaniards also emigrated, to work in countries such as France and Germany.

Today, people are continuing to migrate in their thousands from the four land-locked states of Castilla-León, Castilla-La Mancha, Aragón and Extremadura to the coastal regions. The only exception is Madrid, where the population is increasing each year.

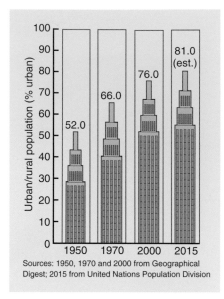

Sources: 1950, 1970 and 2000 from Geographical Digest; 2015 from United Nations Population Division

▲ *The number of people living in urban areas has rapidly increased over the past 50 years.*

◄ *Barcelona, one of the many cities in Spain that has been attracting immigrants from other countries since the mid-1970s.*

IN THEIR OWN WORDS

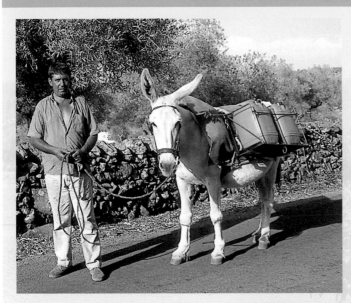

'My name is Juan Gallego. I live in the hills between the small town of Aracena and the border of Portugal in southern Spain. I've lived all my life in the village, farming a small area of land. There are fewer people in our village now than ten years ago – and most of them are old! The young people don't like the idea of the hard work of farming. They leave for the cities to find jobs. Sometimes it bothers me that there aren't many young people around, but most of the time I like the peace and quiet here.'

Immigration

In 2000, nearly 200,000 people, mainly from North Africa, immigrated into Spain. This brought the total number of foreign residents to 938,000 (about 2.7 per cent of the population). There are over 200,000 illegal immigrants from Morocco, by far the largest group from one country.

Spain has made it easier for people to migrate to Spain because of the changing age of the population, and the need for young, manual workers. As the population grows older, Spain faces the prospect of not being able to afford to pay the pensions and healthcare costs of retired people. One of the main banks (BBVA) has calculated that to balance the falling numbers of young people, around 300,000 immigrants need to enter the country every year.

▲ In 2000 Spain opened its frontiers to allow tens of thousands of North Africans to migrate to Spain in order to find work.

Distribution

Spain, with just 80 inhabitants per hectare, is the least densely populated country in Europe, with the exception of Greece. The capital, Madrid, is the most densely populated part of Spain, with more than 600 inhabitants per square kilometre. Otherwise, most of the population is located close to the coasts. The central regions of Castilla-La Mancha, Aragón, Extremadura and Castilla-Leon have large areas with less than 30 people per hectare. These four regions represent 52 per cent of Spain's territory but only 17 per cent of its population. Catalonia occupies just 6 per cent of the national territory, yet accounts for 16 per cent of the population.

This situation has developed over the last thirty years as people have left the countryside in search of jobs and better living conditions. Unlike many European nations, people leaving the countryside have usually headed for urban areas within their own region.

▼ *These children are holidaying in the rural village in the Meseta where they were born. Over the past decade, all their families have moved to Madrid.*

IN THEIR OWN WORDS

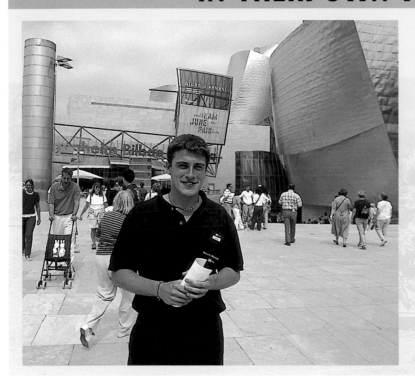

'My name is Eugenio Espinosa and I live in Bilbao. I work in one of the tourist hotels and spend time outside the Guggenheim Museum handing out leaflets to advertise the hotel. I'm a Basque and, like my friends, I'm very proud of what we have achieved here in the Basque country. We were the first area to develop, and today we're one of the most prosperous regions in Spain. I see myself as Spanish, but I'm definitely Basque first and Spanish second.'

A diverse population

Spain is made up of seventeen regions, many with their own distinct cultures and languages. Peoples with very distinctive local identities include the Catalans, Basques and Galicians. In the Basque country, there has been a violent terrorist campaign by a minority group seeking independence from Spain.

There are also over 500,000 Gypsies, or *gitanos*, living in Spain. About half of them live in the south, in Andalucía. Gypsies are believed to have originated in India in the fifteenth century. As in other countries, they have faced poor treatment and discrimination. Many Gypsies have settled to an urban life, but a significant number maintain their traditional roaming lifestyle.

▲ *This Gypsy girl is part of a family that follows the Gypsy tradition of travelling constantly.*

7

Changes at Home

As in most other areas of Spanish society, people's home and family lives have seen big changes since the end of the Franco era. In common with other parts of Europe, over the past few decades the typical Spanish family changed from parents, children, grandparents and other relatives living close to each other in a rural village, to a married couple living with their children in the city.

There has been a rapid decline in the number of marriages since the 1980s. Today, there are fewer marriages in Spain than any EU country other than Sweden. The age at which people first marry has also increased in line with the rest of Europe. The average number of people per household has declined from 4 in 1960 to 3.5 in 1991, and the proportion of single-person households has risen to over 10 per cent.

▶ *Today, young couples enjoy an urban lifestyle and choose to marry later than their parents did.*

IN THEIR OWN WORDS

'My name is Juanita Garcia, and I live in the city of Valladolid, where I'm studying to become a hairdresser. In this picture I'm with my friend, Conchita. I'm on the right. At the weekends, I like to meet up with my friends and stay out until dawn. We want to have fun while we're young. My mother was stuck at home all her life, and I don't want to do the same. I'm looking forward to having a career, and I don't even think about getting married yet! I can't imagine ever having children of my own.'

However, Spain still has a very low divorce rate and few children are born outside of marriage. The percentage of children born to couples who are not married is just 5 per cent in Spain. In comparison, it is 50 per cent in Iceland, Norway and Sweden.

▶ *Men are beginning to take more responsibility for child-rearing. This father is enjoying a meal with his baby daughter.*

Education

In 1975, a good education was generally out of reach of poorer children. Today, the state education offered to the whole population is excellent. School attendance is compulsory for children aged between 6 and 16. The state also provides free schooling for infants between 3 and 5 years of age. In the academic year 1999–2000, 85 per cent of 4-year-olds attended pre-school.

At 14, students can choose one of two paths to follow. There is a two-year course that trains students for specific types of work. Or they can study for the *bachillerato*, an entry qualification for university.

Women

The lives of many women in Spain began to change with the migration of people from the countryside to the urban areas, which started in the 1960s. Life in urban areas offered more freedom for tens of thousands of women. There was a greater number of job opportunities in cities and wages were

▲ *Over the past thirty years it has become easier for people from poorer families to attend university.*

generally higher. Along with greater economic independence, the legal status of Spanish women has improved over the last twenty-five years. Divorce has been legalized, and family planning is widely available. There are now also opportunities for women to work in professions that have previously been exclusively male.

Another great step forward for women was the beginning of compulsory education. The number of women at university has increased dramatically in the last decade. In 1993, just 1.7 per cent of student enrolment for technical institutes and colleges was by women. In 2000, it was up to 40 per cent.

▶ *This young woman has many more opportunities than her mother did. Today, women can be found in almost every area of work.*

IN THEIR OWN WORDS

'I'm Anna Villa Diaz. I live with my family in El Rocio, in Andalucía. When I was young, I wanted to be an agricultural engineer like my father, but he said it was a man's job. After many arguments, he let me go to university to study agriculture. Out of 600 students, there were only about fifty women. I graduated in 1986, and since then there have been a lot of positive changes in the country. Today, men are happy to take my work seriously.'

Religion

For nearly 500 years, Roman Catholicism was the official religion of Spain, and it remains an important part of the lives of most Spanish people. During the time of Franco, between 1939 and 1975, the Church and the government were closely linked. The government even paid the salaries of priests. Until the 1980s, it was possible to get a job in the civil service only if you were a practising Catholic.

Roman Catholicism ceased to be the official religion of Spain in 1977. But around 85 per cent of Spanish people consider themselves to be Catholic, and 40 per cent go to church regularly. Although this is higher than in many southern European countries, it is still a dramatic drop from thirty years ago.

Other religions are also followed in Spain. There are around 350,000 Protestants, mainly in Catalonia. It is estimated that there are more than 400,000 Muslims, mainly people who have moved to Spain from North Africa. There are also around 15,000 Jews.

▲ A child dressed up as part of the Holy Week procession in Aracena. Although many Spanish no longer attend church regularly, they enjoy celebrating traditional holy festivals.

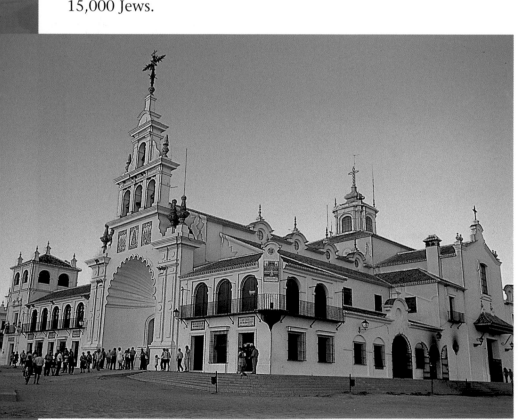

◄ The Ermito del Rocio church in El Rocio houses 'Our Lady of the dew', a statue that attracts worshippers from all over Spain.

Leisure

Only twenty-five years ago Franco controlled entertainment strictly. Few foreign films were permitted, and most celebrations were connected to either the religious or agricultural calendar.

Today, Spanish people are free to enjoy their leisure time in a variety of ways. Football and bullfighting remain the most popular spectator events. Jai Alai is a fast sport from the Basque country, in which contestants use a narrow basket to hurl a small ball or 'pelota' against a wall. Spaniards also enjoy spending time on the beach, and tens of thousands head out of the major cities each summer weekend to the coast. Adventure sports such as white-water canoeing, mountain climbing and mountain biking are increasingly popular.

▶ *The Spanish enjoy outdoor sports. These boys are playing basketball in their local park.*

IN THEIR OWN WORDS

'My name is Diego Perea Garcia and I'm 17 years old. I live in Valencia, but here I am by the Mediterranean Sea near my parents' holiday home in Denia. Denia is a lively town on the Costa Blanca. It's got a medieval castle, a marina and lots of clubs and restaurants.

'I love coming here because there's so much to do. My friends and I go swimming, play football on the beach and ride our scooters. We're lucky because Spain has a sunny climate, so we can spend a lot of our leisure time outdoors.'

Health

Thirty years ago, healthcare in Spain was private and expensive, and located only in the main cities. Where there was public healthcare it was usually only available to people who were in employment, and the quality of treatment was much lower than the private system.

Today, the situation has almost reversed. In the 1980s, Spain began to build a modern health service. Between 1990 and 2000, the percentage of the national economy spent on health has tripled.

However, at 5.5 per cent of the gross domestic product (GDP), this is still slightly below the average expenditure of EU countries (6.6 per cent). Private healthcare is still important, and in

▼ *Older people in Spain have particularly benefited from the improved health service.*

IN THEIR OWN WORDS

'My name is Victor Blasquez. I live in Madrid with my wife and two children. Before my children were born the health system in Spain was not very good. But today the public health service is considered better than the private. People still use private hospitals for minor surgery, but for specialist treatment of serious illness the best doctors work in the public hospitals. We're lucky, because in the capital there are many hospitals and doctors. In the countryside some people still have to travel long distances for treatment.'

1999 approximately 6.3 million people had private medical insurance. For specialist medical care, though, state hospitals are now considered to offer a better quality of care.

Diet

Traditional foods – fish, olives, cereals and wine – remain the major components of the Spanish diet. The new forms of horticulture mean that fresh fruit and vegetables are now available even in the winter months. As in most Western countries, fast food such as burgers and pizzas is becoming more popular among young people. However, the traditional Spanish tapas, where small plates of food are served as snacks alongside drinks, remains a favourite across the generations. Many regions have their own special dishes.

▲ *Fresh fruit has always been an important part of the Spanish diet, and with the introduction of new farming methods it can now be eaten all year round.*

◄ *Spanish families enjoy eating at tapas bars such as this one in the marina in Barcelona.*

8 Changes at Work

Once a mainly agricultural society, Spain now has an economy dominated by service industries such as tourism, banking and commerce. It is also a major manufacturing country, and since joining the EU in 1986 has increased its trade with other members. The growth of service industries has been accompanied by a sharp decline in the number of people working in agriculture and fisheries – although this took place much later than in most other European countries. In 2000, agriculture and fisheries accounted for just 3.6 per cent of GDP.

▼ An increasing number of people are finding work in the tourism industry. This modern science park in Valencia is a major tourist attraction and employs hundreds of local people.

Manufacturing

Spain's manufacturing industries have changed rapidly since the country became part of the EU. They have moved from the more traditional heavy industries of textiles and steel to newer, high-tech industries. Because of the lower salaries paid to Spanish workers, many foreign companies have invested in Spain.

Spain's single most important manufacturing industry is vehicle production, which accounted for around 6 per cent of the total GDP in 2000. In that year, Spain produced more than 3 million vehicles for the first time. It is now the fifth-largest vehicle producer in the world. However, none of the large vehicle companies that operate in Spain are Spanish-owned. The car manufacturer SEAT, for example, is owned by Volkswagen, a German company.

The other leading industrial sectors are energy production, oil refining, chemical production and food processing. The construction industry is more important in Spain than in neighbouring countries. This is partly due to the demand for tourist accommodation.

▲ A petrochemical plant at Huelva. The production of chemicals is a major industry in Spain.

IN THEIR OWN WORDS

'My name is Dani Medina and I enjoy writing my own programs and designing games on my computer. I'm studying hard to go to university, but I'm interested in industry rather than computers. I think there will soon be too many people wanting jobs in computer programming. I can learn computing by myself, and I will always be able to use my computer skills in my spare time or as part of my work. Spain's manufacturing industry is really strong, and I think my chances of finding work in this area are strong. I'd like to get good qualifications so that I don't have to start right at the bottom!'

Agriculture

The importance of agriculture in the Spanish economy has declined sharply in the last decade. But Spain remains one of the most important agricultural and fishing nations in Europe. Crops are produced much more efficiently today than they were in the 1970s and 1980s, and this has been at the cost of many jobs. In 1976, 2.6 million people were involved in agriculture and fishing. By 2000, the number had fallen below 1 million.

Spain is the world's largest producer of olive oil, and Europe's third-largest producer of wine. The production of sugar and beef has been threatened by cheap imports. However, the country's climate is ideal for irrigated horticulture, and over the past ten years the quantity of fruit and vegetables grown under plastic, such as tomatoes and strawberries, has grown considerably. It now accounts for around 25 per cent of agricultural output.

Much of Spain's agriculture is very labour intensive. For example, olives are harvested by hand. As young people leave the countryside to find better-paid jobs in the cities, there is less labour available. So in future this type of agriculture may well rely on migrant workers.

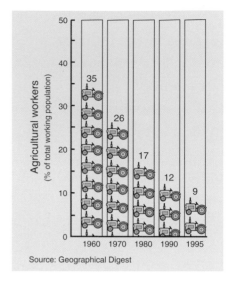

Source: Geographical Digest

▲ *The number of people working in agriculture fell dramatically from 1960 to 1995.*

▶ *Today, many younger people are discouraged from farming by the hard manual labour involved. This man is transporting harvested cork oak by hand.*

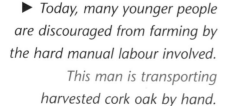

Fisheries

Although it has the biggest fishing fleet in Europe, Spain's fishing industry is in decline. It employs 75,000 fishermen, mainly in the north-west of the country and the southern region of Andalucía. Half of Spain's 2,000 commercial fishing boats are located in the region of Galicia, and these account for 70 per cent of the national catch. The EU is placing restrictions on all fishing activities in an attempt to protect declining fish populations. This means that there is far less work available in the fishing industry than there was in the past.

▼ *A catch of sardines is unloaded in the southern port of Barbate. Both fish stocks and the Spanish fishing fleet are in decline.*

IN THEIR OWN WORDS

'My name is Alfonso Gonzalez. I work as a fisherman on the southern coast. In the last ten years the sardines have been harder and harder to find. We're spending more time at sea and catching less. The same is true of most of the boats in the harbour. The only boats that are making good money are the ones that bring in yellow-fin tuna from the new fish farms off the coast. It's very sad to watch our industry shrinking. The EU is trying to improve things, but our job is very difficult at the moment.'

Service industries

Service industries include banking, tourism, catering and computer programming, as well as public services such as health, education and garbage collection. Spain's economy is similar to all modern industrialized countries in that its service sector employs more people than all the other sectors combined. It accounts for around two-thirds of the total national economy (65.9 per cent of GDP).

▼ *The boom in tourism has led to many people leaving agriculture to work in hotels such as this one in Zahara de los Atunes.*

Tourism

Tourism is an extremely important part of Spain's economy. Spain was the first country to develop mass tourism, and during the 1960s and 1970s tourism expanded rapidly. Since the Olympic Games in Barcelona, tourist numbers have climbed to a new record high in 2000

IN THEIR OWN WORDS

'My name is David Requelme and I work in a hotel in Jimena de la Frontera, in Andalucía. In a job like mine, you meet lots of interesting people. I can also practise my English and French. Although it's hard work, it's much better than working on a farm. Hardly any young people want to do that sort of work these days. If it wasn't for jobs in hotels and as guides, most young people would leave the area.'

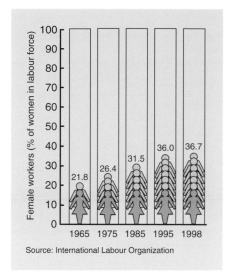

of 48.2 million foreign visitors. That is more than the entire population of the country. Spain is now the third most important tourist destination in the world after France and the USA. In 2000, tourism earned Spain over US $30 million.

Women at work

As Spain's population has become increasingly urban, opportunities for women have increased rapidly. Up until the end of the Franco era, women accounted for less than 25 per cent of the working population. Today, the figure is approaching 40 per cent. In addition, the type and quality of work available to women has changed. Most parts of the economy, and in particular the growing service sector, offer opportunities for women. It is common now for senior positions in law firms, banks and other service sector professions to be occupied by women.

Source: International Labour Organization

▲ *An ever-increasing number of Spanish women are joining the workforce.*

◄ *Women now have a strong presence in the Spanish workforce, even in traditionally male jobs. This young woman is a miner in Asturias.*

The Way Ahead

At the frontier of Europe and Africa, Spain is in an ideal position to increase trade with the developing economies of Africa. Spain is benefiting from being a member of the European Union, and the future of the economy looks strong.

However, not everyone is sharing in Spain's prosperity. Remote villages are inhabited largely by poor and elderly people, with the young migrating to cities. Poorer people in cities like Barcelona are being forced out of the city centres, because property prices are increasing as old buildings are restored with EU money.

Living standards have improved dramatically in Spain in the last twenty-five years, and the country has one of the highest life expectancies in the world. But over the next

◀ The European flag flies alongside Spain's national flag and the regional flag of Catalonia in the town of Lleida. The future of Spain depends on its different regions working together and Spain continuing to play an active role in the EU.

IN THEIR OWN WORDS

'I'm Veronica Merino and I'm 17 years old. I'm studying in Madrid to enter the Guarda Civil, which is like the FBI in the United States. It's very difficult to be accepted. You have to study for two years, and spend three more years at a special training camp. If I succeed I'm guaranteed a job for life, and women can now reach the highest ranks. I think life in Spain is getting better all the time, and I'm looking forward to the future.'

thirty years, the population is set to decline. There will be many more old people to care for, and by 2030 more than 80 per cent of the population will live in urban areas. These changes mean that more migrants, especially from North Africa, will be needed in Spain to make up the shortfall in agricultural workers.

Spain has enough land to maintain its economic activities and keep its wilderness areas. But its developing infrastructure – its highways, irrigation systems and dams – and the 48 million tourists who visit each year, may have a serious effect on the environment. The coasts need to be protected to ensure the long-term success of the tourist industry. One of Spain's biggest challenges for the future is to exploit its resources while at the same time conserving them.

▲ *Tourists enjoy the spectacular architecture of the new science park in Valencia. As well as building new attractions, Spain must ensure that it protects its stunning natural environment.*

Glossary

Agriculture Farming the land and producing food.

Arid Dry land in which there is low rainfall and little plant life.

Biodiversity The variety of plant and animal species in a particular habitat.

Birth rate The number of people born in a given area over a period of time.

Cordillera Mountain range.

Deforestation The clearance of forest areas.

Democracy A system of government in which the population vote for the person or party who will govern them.

Dictator A person who rules a country with little or no regard for the wishes of the country's citizens.

Drought A long period when there is very little rain, or no rain at all.

Economy All the business activity in a country.

Emigrate To go to live in another country.

Export To sell goods to another country.

Extinction When an animal or plant species no longer exists.

Faction A group of people who act together to achieve a particular goal.

Franco era The time between 1939 and 1975 when the dictator General Francisco Franco ruled Spain.

Gross national product (GNP) The value of all goods and services produced by a country during a certain period.

Horticulture A type of agriculture that specializes in fruit and vegetables.

Hydrocarbons Substances that contain carbon, oxygen and hydrogen. This usually refers to coal or oil.

Hydroelectric power Electricity generated by using the power of water.

Immigration Coming to live in a country from abroad.

Imports Goods that are bought from another country.

Irrigation systems Pipes and channels set up to supply water to crops.

Life expectancy How long people in a given area are expected to live.

Manufacturing Making goods.

Meseta A tableland or plateau.

Migrants People who move from one place to live in another, either within a country or between countries.

Mineral A hard substance, such as coal, that can be mined.

Nuclear power Electricity made from the energy of splitting atoms.

Petrochemicals Chemicals made from oil.

Plateau A high flat area of land.

Population The total number of people in a place at a given time.

Rural Countryside.

Service sector The part of an economy that is involved in providing services rather than making goods.

Soil erosion When the amount of soil in a particular area rapidly decreases.

Subsidies Government money that is given to a particular group to help with a specific project.

Urban Built-up, as in a town or city.

Wetlands Areas in which the soil has a very high water content, such as a swamp.

Further Information

Books

Spain: a History by Raymond Carr
(Oxford University Press, 2000)

Next Stop Spain by Fred Martin
(Heinemannn Library, 1998)

Lonely Planet: Spain by Damien Simonis
(Lonely Planet Publications, 2001)

Spain and the Spanish
(Franklin Watts)

Useful addresses

Spanish Tourist Office
22-23 Manchester Square
London W1U 3PY
Tel: 020 7486 8077

Anglo-Spanish Society
96 St. Albans Avenue
London W4 5JR
Tel: 020 8995 8463

Spanish Embassy
39 Chesham Place
London SW1X 8SB
Tel: 020 7235 5555

Spanish Education Office, Spanish Embassy
20 Peel St
London W8 7PD
Tel: 020 7727 2462

Websites

http://www.odci.gov/cia/publications/factbook
Information about Spain from the CIA
Factbook, including information about
Spanish geography, population, economy
and politics.

http://www.photius.com/wfb2000/countries/
spain/spain_geography.html
Geographical information about Spain,
including maps and flags.

http://www.sispain.org
An interactive website containing information
about most aspects of Spain and Spanish life,
including history, the environment, health
and education.

Index

Numbers in **bold** are pages where there is a photograph or illustration.

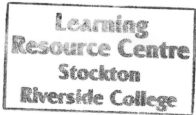